THE COLORS OF LIFE

In the Beginning God said "Let There Be Light"
The knowledge of light can be enhancement to
life and the over standing of how light and color
have an effect on it. These writing are to enlighten
the readers on light, colors and how the
knowledge of what we see and feel yet do not
understand have influences we do not readily
recognize. Thinking deeply on creation and how it
all got started we have to take the beginning
literally. God said let there be light! This is not
only a very important statement, it draws the
question, why light? What is the importance or
significance of light? We use light to see in
everyday life. We need light to see what we are
doing be it work or play. What is the propose for
God to command light to appear in the universe
first. Is there a hidden power to light? If we unlock
the power of light how will it affect us. Is thIs a
source from source energy that only source
energy can control? This could be one of the main
powers of the Gods, the knowledge and the use of
source energy. We first must understand to over
stand what light is and how we perceive it.

Frist we need some knowledge of the nature of light. Light is a form of energy called electromagnetic radiation. This radiation comes in waves, frequency and intensity. The frequency and intensity of this light can be measured in what is known as wavelengths. The light is seen in waves and the frequency of the wave will produce determined the wavelength. Wavelengths determines the hue or color we see. The intensity of the frequency determines the visual sensation that cause brightness and color to be perceived. We perceive these frequencies though are eyes. It is important to over stand the how the eye works and how we responses to the sensations received and perceived by the frequencies. These frequencies and wavelengths are previewed through the eye as color. The eye in this case solve the problem of converting the energy of light from wavelengths it is projecting and perceived. The work of the eye to provide vision requires separating the foreground from the background, recognizing objects presented in a variety of orientation and situation and accurately interpreting the information. Vision begins the second the eye focuses light on the retina where it is absorbed through a layer of photoreceptors cells. These cells convert light into electrochemical signals that are divided into two parts, rods and cones. Rod and cones are named for their shape and duties. The eye has two fluid chambers. Light passes through the clear cornea into the first chamber. The cones are concentrated in the center of the retina called the fovea and are responsible for high acuity tasks like reading and color vision. Cones are the protective coating on the surface of the eye that light passes through to the iris. The iris is colored and opens and closes to regulate how light passes through the pupil into the lens. The lenses are the transparent portion of the eye that focuses light on the Retina. The lens is held in place by ligaments that are attached to the Ciliary muscle. The Ciliary muscle focuses images by controlling the thickness of the lens making a clear image fall on the light sensitive Retina at the back of the second chamber. At the back of the chamber the retina breaks down the light waves with two types of receptors. These receptors are called Rods and cones. There are about 120 million cell located outside the center of the retina that transduce light waves into neural impulses that code information about light and dark called Rod. Rods work differently than cones in four ways. For one the one of the rods responsibility is peripheral vision which is focus on the top bottom and sides off the visual field. Rods are responsible for night vision and dim reflections as well as your peripheral vision. The rods are much more sensitive too light than cones they can pick up information in dim light which produce images that are perceived less visual acute because the neurons converge that their impulse are sent to the brain on a single nerve fiber called the optic nerve. The optic nerve routes the information to the brains hypothalamus to the cerebral cortex where the actual visual perception that's place. The Cone however is more commonly send their messages to the brain along separate nerve fibers giving a much more precise image and information about the location of the stimulation on the retina. There ae about 6 million of these type of receptor cells located in the center of the retina that transduce light waves into neural impulses also coding information about light and dark and code information about color. Color vision is the energy produce in a wavelength within the spectrum of visual light that evokes a sensation from a specific color when stimulated received and perceived by the human visual system. The Color is produced by the intensity of the energy within the frequency perceived in life. Thus color has an impact on us and in our daily life. The brain processes this information received by the eye and relates the sensation to the mind and body. Colors seem to influence our perception that which in part control our emotion and our situational reactions to the stimuli and atmosphere. The eyes pick up the light reflected decoding various wavelengths into color signals that are than transmitted to the brain where it is interpreted as a specific color that we receive, perceive and response to. Every color has a unique effect on individuals and stimulates responses. Colors can also have differing effects and responses on male and females. For a better look at this, a color like dark green may have a motivational effect on a man whereas the color pink will stimulate a response from a woman compared to a color like red or blue which will stimulate basically the same preprogramed responses for men and women that trigger the subconscious mind that evokes your memory and reaction to the stimuli. The memory and responses are stored or programed in the brain as well as the heart. The body has many different types chemicals, receptors, processors and transmitters that operate throughout the human body. For the purpose of showing the effect of color on the human mind and body, we will limit the defining to describe the necessary components to view the cause and effects colors can have on human life and how we perceive it. The eyes are the tools of the two the two central organs and their two separate and induvial operating systems. For now, we will focus on the way these operating systems with perception intelligence, work with the eyes to perceive color and the reaction to the reflection we perceive through the eye. Frist and foremost, lets over stand that the brain and the heart work together to create an experience that is committed to memory based on the stimuli it perceives with the use of the eyes. The heart continually transmits its emotional signals to the brain which sends back coded information to the heart want the brain perceived which send the vibration and frequency back to the heart. It has been confirmed studies that document the biological signal the heart transmits to the brain through the blood stream coded information in a protein molecule called a neuropeptide. The brain transmitters these and other signal through the whole body that produce the vibration from the perception that causes the emotions that lead to the preprogrammed thought or reaction. The perceived emotion from the vibration created by the stimuli, in this case color, can cause emotions of Love, hate, fear, joy, which is felt though the body and can evoke thought or meditation. They can also be used to deprogram and/or reprogram the human mind. We will travel deeper into this line of thought later in this writing thus we will continue to look at the cycle that cause the reactions from the perception perceived by color. In our unconscious state of being our subconscious in at work in the back of the mind and is what fuels our automatic reaction to all things. As to a detailed functions of the subconscious mind, we will limit this topic to how it applies to color and its effects. The eyes, brain and heart enter into this cycle that they get used to by replaying the stimuli and reaction causing the reputation of a certain experience on a regular basis until it is committed to memory. These instructions have been implanted in the mind throughout life. As adults for example in our teen age year we all wanted to learn to drive a car. There are laws and rules you must follow when operating a motor vehicle as well as learning how to handle the vehicle itself. In learning the law one of the things taught in a driver's safety class in street signs and light signals. We will have learned that red means stop, green means go and yellow means to move with caution. As we learned the meaning of the colors we also learned the action we should take when we see these signals. We learnt that if we see a red light in are path or roadway we are to react by bring the vehicle to a stop and when the light turns green are reaction is to go while the yellow indicates that you should continue with caution. This cycle becomes implanted in the subconscious of the mind and repeated automatically in this cycle we will call habit for now.

Types

There are many colors, sometime spelled colour, for the purpose of this writing this book we will use the spelling, COLOR, color comes in many shades and pigments. Color can be mixed with other colors to create new colors. Merriam-Webster defines it as a phenomenon of light or visual perception that enables one to differentiate otherwise identical objects. (red, brown, pink, or gray) are some of the examples of colors. Colors have been used for different reasons with different meanings, there can be used as a warning or signal and can also be used to identify a group or organization. Combinations of colors have been assembled in a unique fashion to represent their country or state. They have also been known as symbols. One symbol we will look at is the one given by the highest Creator of Pure Source, God, that came with a promise. The symbol, series and collection of colors we know as a rainbow is the sign God uses continually to remind mankind if the time the waters covered the earth. The promise is that He will never cover or destroy the earth again with rain and water. It is in these colors we find much more than a symbol or views that are pleasant to look at or used for the identification objects that would be difficult to differentiate. These color have power; these colors have keys to some of the secrets in life. A little known fact is that colors have their own frequencies and vibration that can be controlled to produce different effects of perception. The effect of the perception of these realities may have impact on the lives of those who and use the principles of colors and its frequencies. We are going to look at some of the colors known to mankind as the rainbow that glows and always shows the blessing from God that we have all heard of. (the Lesson from Above) these colors have power, meaning and uses that go beyond that symbol of the covenant between The Highest Source of Power and life. These are color that share some secrets in life. the colors consist of Red, Yellow, Green, Orange, Blue, Indigo and Violet. Each color has its own frequency, vibration and effect. We will take a look at some of these colors, that have some direct or effect and some of their effects.

We will start with what we will call the it colors model which is an attempt to standardize the color attributes and how to show their basic interrelation by some color theorists. These are as follows, Red to Orange to yellow to green to blue to purple and red once again. This is almost likening to the musical scale of do-ray-me-fa-so-la-tee-do. Liken to the sound of music color too returns to it place of origination. Colors are specific wavelengths from a visible light spectrum reflected or transmitted by an object, reflection or filtration.

Colors

RED

Red has a frequency wavelength measured in nanometers, at roughly 620-740 of visible light. Red, a dominate color is known for many attributes, symbols and signs. Red has a positive effect on memory by improving one's focus by drawing your attention to it. Red is a color that symbolizes Love and research suggest that men are more attracted to women wearing red feeling a sensation of they think may be love. Red is one of the more preferred color and picked as a favorite color by most people. Red is one of the most vibrate and invigorating of the active colors and stimulates a mindset that triggers the adrenal gland to send information through the neurons leading a response. These responses can cause changes in your metabolism increasing your blood circulation and breathing rate. Red can take on a variety and is associated with love and war with the strong ability to track attention. People who gravitate toward the color red ae usually high energy personality type of people. This type of person will show extroverted tendencies naturally and those who chose the color tend to make choses to show or prove their spirit. People who have chosen the color because it symbolizes to them the way they would like to be seen by others. To try and shine in the brightness of its glair in hopes to share it the braveness of strength and courage the color signifies. The natural has this energy in life alone. It is life and the light that comes with it that provide their level of energy. They live happy exciting lives with positive attitudes toward all of life and the adventures that lay within.

ORANGE- While not as bold or heavy as the color red, the color orange has it ability to attract a more playful energy show us its vibrancy and vitality and produces an atmosphere of a playful impulse in a healthy environment. The color Orange occurs between the colors Red and Yellow in the visible spectrum and can be described as a warm cheerful lamination of color. The frequency vibration that this color projects is a balanced wavelength that sends signals of calmness, not too happy and joyous as a type of the color red naturally would be categorizes, but cheerful and having a feeling of bliss accompanies the attitude of this personality. These people tend to be peace a caring to all human beings, tall or small they like us all. This type of person stays with a consentient flow of positive energy filled with good karma. Those people draw to the color orange are more influenced by a steady vibration that could give them the cultural titles as The Nice People, The

People of Peace or The Children of God. All of these descriptive titles would fit these people well. YELLOW - yellow is a different type of color and may seem strange to some because of the type of changes it can take you through. The color can be associated with the smiling buttons that some people wear to show others people their mood of happiness and joy. Like the color red and orange, yellow has its own ability to stimulate and vitalize positive and/or negative connotation when the color activate anxiety in the center of the brain when perceived as a cautionary signal. Yellow is seen between the frequency of Green and Orange and is sometime used to symbolize gold and the sun of this earth as well as the recollection of summers passed. Yellow has its power to effect humans in a number of ways and applications. This color can have an effect on the mental and spiritual level causing an introspective focus. Yellow stimulates a chemical in the brain called serotonin also known as 5-hydroxytryptamine. This chemical comes from the amino acid tryptophan and works as a neurotransmitter in areas in the brain like the hypothalamus. Inactivity of this chemical can cause mental disorders like depression. The serotonin in the body needs to be kept in balance and the color yellow aids in this, you can say this is one of the active light of God projected and received in color. When balanced the serotonin in the brain enhanced by the color yellow could be responsible for improved concentration and activates a heighten sense of alertness of the nerves systems awareness that response to the stimuli of the situation. GREEN - Green, a part of the sub active color system rides between Blue and Yellow that evoke a predominate wavelength of roughly 495-570 nanometers. Let's go green is a phase you hear a lot nowadays. Thinking of the environment, nature and life in an attempt to save the planet earth. This makes green more than a color it is a direction a way of life chosen by people that have be inspired to make changes in the way they and other live life. As with nature green is a natural color that has stable attributes. The color green actives a relaxing feeling for those how encounter this eye pleasing color. Green has a healing hygienic effect when it triggers the brain to start, recognizing green as a color that represents growth and life. BLUE- Whereas Blue vibrates between Violet and Green on the optical spectrum of visible light producing a frequency of 450- 495 nanometers. Blue also has an effect on the mind and body of human beings. Blue too has the ability to active chemicals in the brain that can have a calming response that help unlock creative, peaceful mind set. Blue serve as a popular color for safety and security, it is a refreshing look and It symbolizes blue skies and wide open ocean views that lead to a peaceful relaxing feeling from the chemicals they release in the mind that transmit itself through the nerve center of the brain. Attributes associated with this color are trustworthy, inviting, serene, it's a boy and loyalty to name a view (could not resist the word play "view" for "few"). The color blue evokes the feeling of safety and strength and call the favorite color chosen by millions of people worldwide.

INDIGO-   Indigo this color takes on more than one color name as its hue can slightly change in degrees of depth as in the color names purple, violet or lavender. These are subtle colors that are associated with elegance. People drawn in these color usually sensitive and have above average tastes and expectation thus liking the finer thing in life such as fine arts, lace clothes, paintings and pottery, the ballet and symphony and other believed to be refined pursuits. Indigo is more of the spiritual aspects of this color.

Realizing Color

Take the time to stop and think, do we really pay attention to color on a daily basis. Can you conceive or even image the world without color? It seems that most of the time we do not see color as color but something we react to as thought and /or programing. Yet Color play a very important role I our everyday life and has proven to be the cause of human response, activities and emotion are greatly influenced by them. The majority of the people who walk around daily reacting to the stimuli of color are unaware of the effect color has on their everyday lives. Our bodies absorb the frequencies from color and starts it process of informing the mind the information its receives from the particular color through the eyes and transmits the preprogramed information to the body part or emotion to cause a response or reaction.

The heart sense these transmitted signal that are created in the brain and send the information or message to a molecule called neuropeptides and transmits it through the bodies blood stream.

When the heart senses and /or receive the information from a particular color it creates a certain type of neuropeptide. For example, when the eye views the color red it sends a message to stop if you are driving or walking or doing some type of action. Given another situation where one is placed in a red room one may become easily aggravated or violent whereas when the brain received the information that the color is orange or yellow the brain will send a message of joy, happiness and fun. The type of information the neuropeptide cell received by the brain, from the heart creates interpretations and perception in the form of images, action, reaction and emotions that affect us yet we are unaware of the preprogramed thought. For example, a person in a room in the color Blue may be draw to a mental state of creative though. The vibration created by the brain because of these perceptions are felt in the human body and access by the heart which produces more neuropeptide of the same type to send back to the into the brain. The focus of our unaware awareness create the message sent to the body caused by the stimuli. These repeated reactions and actions create a cycle of thought, action, reactions and emotions.

Programing by way of repetition implants in the brain the responding action, reaction and emotional behavior we as human exhibit. In one way of thought the brain and mind become addicted to these patterns. The brain is always cycling, recycling and replacing brain cells. When it comes to replacing brain cell, the brain will replace a cell type of the neuropeptide with a new cell that the brain itself programs to fit into the cycle and system that it gets regularly of the heart. This designs the new brain cell with a higher receptivity to that particular neuropeptide. Your brain gets use to cells with strong and frequently repeated patterns having receptivity to certain stimuli. Color acts as a source of stimuli creating a pattern of behavior based on the stimuli or color. To make it easier to digest Repeated action, reaction and emotion processed by the brain get programed to your subconscious mind. Realistically that sub conscious mind is no more than a neural pathway were the reactions to certain stimuli based on what had been established in your brain as a result of past conditioning. This is what we meant by the colours of life. The impact color has on the human mind without the individual people realize that they are acting on programed instinct. This is from and for what we perceive from the visual, physical colors see by eye human eye. There are colors that exist that are not seen by the human eye that stay around us.

Aura

 Though the ages people of spiritual awareness have been known to see colour around individual people and objects. Each of us is surrounded by our own individual rainbow of colors not seen by the human eye. These vibrating bands of colors from this field of energy is vibrating at wavelengths ranges level not visible with normal physical vision. We cannot see these vibration of color because it is moving or vibrating either too fast or too slow to come into the ranges of human sight. Remembering color has been defined as wavelength of light vibrating at certain frequencies divided in spectrums of rays. Each has different characteristics producing sensation on the retina of the eye which is interpreted as color to the brain. Simplified color is what our sense perceives between light and drack. Between what can be seen and what cannot be seen, the visible and the invisible. Color is where the human being is touched, comes in contact with and experiences creation. Color is being change takes place and change is the only constant factor to the universe. When color reflects or is absorb it goes into an energy system of sorts. For this writing we will stay with the effects on the human body and mind. Absorb though the retina of the eye and the processes that lead to the brain, body and mind it is applied to the human energy system. Thus color not only effects the appearance of thing it effects the energy system it comes in contact with having a psychological effect on us all as individual people and in a programed group. Some people are very sensitive to the wavelengths not readily seen by human being yet see these rays of light and color that surround people. These light and color are known as auras. This is also a practice and art form known by many spiritual practitioners known by some as shaman how have attune their mind to pick up frequencies not normally seen with the human eye. Remember most of the action, reaction and emotion to color go on unrealized by people. Those how have stop and started paying attention to the character of color and the reaction to them have been able to change or reprogram their mind from the programed action, reaction and emotion when they come to contact with different colors. They see the light and dark as yin and yang, white and black, like positive and negative and a spectrum between. The positive light/white/yang side of the spectrum represent force and spirit whereas The negative dark/black/yin side of the spectrum represent passiveness and absorbs energy of light and color. This put the color red on the light/yang side of the spectrum moving more Intune with the physical frequencies with a shorter wavelength then   the color indigo/ violet/yin which has a longer polarity and a slower vibration and id more spiritual. To a Shaman, in the eye they have an ear whereas color had sound and color and sound are aspect of the same thing, the movement or vibration of energy. To the Shaman sound is a color they can hear each color has its own tune, its very own sound and these sounds have different points in the body that response to them. These points in the body that the frequency of sound from light are called chakras. Chakra have set point in the human body and are signaled by the sensation from the stimuli and distributed through your body. Each of these chakra have a color that is associates with it. Each chakra has its own function and purpose that are over stand by these shamans through what they call "Spiritual Healing" where they use color, sound and light to realigned the chakras to bring freedom from the mental, subconscious programed reactions and emotion they have come to repeat and act on without being aware as to way. Freeing the mind from programed and preprogramed mental habit is one of the first step in reprograming the subconscious mind with self-prescribed information and messaging to be triggered by the same stimuli that cause your preprogram reaction and emotions. These chakra points in the body start as the frequencies to color line up. We will start again with the color red, the root chakra the first of this energy center which is the densest and the base of this energy center. Red is the slowest wavelength of the spectrum yet the most stimulating color. The power from the color pull the retina forward and draws the focus of our attention on whatever object or situation at that present time. Red is the color of our life force and energy itself. It is also associated with the Adrenal Gland which is associated with the survival response of "fight or flight" instinct. Next in the line of chakra point in the body is the Sacral Chakra and is associated with the color Orange and is located below the navel and is a color and chakra of creativity, vitality and strength, a warm color associated with the sun. This chakra is located in the pelvic area and know to stimulate wisdom and a path to growth and development. The third energy center is located in the Solar Plex and is associated with the color yellow, the color of the sun and is the core of our being a fill the mind with hope and optimism. The chakra the has the element of healing in found in the heart and has the energy of love, peace, tranquility and transformation This allows you to transform your ego to attune to the lower chakras and aligns with the other chakras. Blue, one of the three primary colors and is the color associated with the Throat Chakra and is known for is ability to communicate. Blue energy is calming, healing and lend itself to the thoughts of a sky blue Haven itself. The sixth chakra in this color connected version of light having visual sound power to activate the energy system of the body is the all seeing Eye Chakra, opening one awareness and consciousness of oneness and spirituality. Associated with the night this royal blue of the third eye is thought to be a pathway to the divine, the bridge between Heaven and earth, the connector of human and spirit, the connection of the right and left hemispheres of the brain and its activities. Last on this physical, mental, spiritually comic journey is the unifying Crown Chakra. Violet offers the emotion of wholeness, a oneness with all life in the physical and mental worlds we live in. Shaman over standing these principles can apply the knowledge to undo what has been done and unlock one mind to find different realities in life and the ability to change the effect that The Colours of life has on our everyday lives.

www.ingramcontent.com/pod-product-compliance
Lightning Source LLC
Chambersburg PA
CBHW050933290526
45792CB00002B/994